R Some Music And A Little War

Other Poetry by Peter Finch

Wanted — Second Aeon 1968
Pieces of the Universe — Second Aeon 1969
Cycle of the Suns — Art Living 1970
Beyond the Silence — Vertigo 1970
An Alteration in the Way I breathe — QWO 1970
The Edge of Tomorrow — BB Books 1971
The End of the Vision — John Jones Cardiff Ltd 1971
Whitesung — Aquila 1972
Antarktika — Writers Forum 1972
Blats — Second Aeon 1973
Trowch Eich Radio 'mlaen — Writers Forum 1977
Connecting Tubes — Writers Forum 1980
Big Band Dance Music — Balsam Flex 1980
Visual Texts 1970-80 — Pyrofiche 1981
The O Poems — Writers Forum 1981
Blues and Heartbreakers — Galloping Dog 1981
Dances Interdites — Balsam Flex 1982

Some Music and a Little War

Peter Finch

 Rivelin Grapheme Press
London & Bradford 1984

For Val

Acknowledgements

Some of these poems, often in earlier versions, have appeared in the following: *Element 5, Strange Mathematics, Il Cobold, Wordsworth, Green Horse, Anglo-Welsh Review, The Fault* (USA), *Dharma* (Australia), *Now* (Jamaica), *Eureka* (Sweden), *Caret, Transatlantic Review, Maximum Load, The Beau, Reality Studios, Spectrum, Slow Dancer* and *Stand*.

Contents

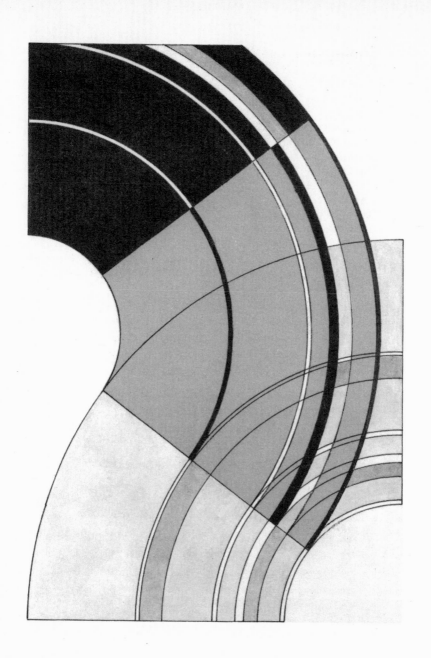

Encounter

It was the length of the grass
that caught them

both obvious and unexpected

they grappled easily,
bucking, shouting,
                    roaring some.
Took mouths of air
as if to demonstrate
                    their superiority

it was a tedious encounter

and as time and water
bent their bones
they turned to stutter
slow teeth and seed and stalk

in the end they became almost human
watching each others eyes
for that flicker of bestiality

it was a strange day
with the sun like a thunderbolt
rolling amongst the clouds
the grass yellow thin,
tall, and full of miles

a day for the meeting of lions

obviously.

Darkness and the Sounds of Water

six sodium moons
in the river,
six silent satellites
of glass and gas

the real moon lies flickering
and I watch it crack
where waters twist
and the heavy froth
is yellow
       for a moment
before black.

I listen for my breath,
hear only water,
and the sounds
          of the dawn
coming back.

Box

Box
green box
the common box
box beyond the bladdernut
oval box
glossy box
the widespread, abundant box
the box far on from the spindle
hairless, pale belly, one-sexed,
box the tropical
its clusters edging the buckthorn
its sight on the lime and the vine
box the persistent curved one
the stouter one, the larger one
box of the spanish main.
its fruits worrying the tamarisk
its flower a spyglass to the dogwood
its style famous in the honeysuckle
box the widespread, the 4-angled,
the one of even grain
slowly
box growing
scuffing drylands
tangling rain.

A Piece for Bob Cobbing on his Sixtieth Birthday

long tomes

rattling half spines

insistent flow

This man has teeth. He is a mighty man.
He waves his arms for music. He is always
standing. We are always falling down.

Seam on seam

ska screws

rolling mill

Black earth, rain, leaves. A memory
of how it must have been. His garden
has the shards of sculpture, elongated
echoes, brown ghosts, trickles of
time.

tape tappet

silent evolution

his triumph

One sunday he forgot where he was.
Woke in pitch, dark tunnel, sweating,
wires and frail jewellery, out under the
road. Emerged in amber, drumming, mantric
sound.

his name changed
birds flew behind his eyes

scratched the name of god
a thousand times

chirping

crackle

This man has arms. He is a music man.
He waves his teeth for might. He is always
winning. We are always burning down.

familiar skies

buddhist small talk

swings,
it almost rattles

He is on a hillside, above the trees.
He can hear animals breathing.
He is an amplifier. They are sheep.
They are drunk. The landscape dances.

This man has dreams. He is an honourable
man. He waves his head for music. He is
always singing. We are always spinning
round.

An Idea of Empire

(In 1870 Col. Wolseley took a British force, by river, 660 miles across almost impassable forest territory to subdue the Metis at Fort Garry in central Canada. When he reached his destination the encampment was deserted and taken without the firing of a shot.)

God's soldier
on this heathen water,
Garnet Joseph Wolseley,
Colonel,
sea behind him.

He puts his eye
to the surface,
watches it slowly swell.
In the lake of woods
he sees the interface
between hull
and algae,
stonewort, sponge,
moss snail, flatworm,
fluke.

He is an army by himelf,
vociferous,
in permanent rage.

He is disgusted by dampness,
snails, fungi,
water plantains,
arums, bur-reeds,
flowering rush.

He catches leeches in
a jar. Down with drink forgets,
sees them as fruit,
blueberries, raisins, pieces of plum. He rams
them in his mouth like nuts. This food,
he says, is women's work. Brings it all
back on the buckled bank.

On water
he imagines himself invincible
newt
toad
three-spined stickleback.

There he is with his
bright red-jackets,
an army
of very English men.

If there was an option
they'd all go back to Ottawa
and drink.
This rainwater
and religion
is no fullfillment
for healthy men.

Col. Wolseley remembering his
purpose. Squeezing the brackish
river from the leather of his boots.
He has fire in his eyes.
"Melt the forest," they shout,
"take us on wheels, on cushions,
feather us, blow us, sail us on
through to the plains."

Wolseley has a man
to wave away the flies,
a gesticulator like windmill,
amid the encroaching swarms.

Mayflies,
stoneflies,
black flies,
bugs,
two winged demons,
biting mouth parts,
red marks on his skin.

"Men," he bawls,
"we will blow out this dominion
like a balloon.

We will be axe-men,
swordsmen, champions of light.
We will carry her forwards,
victorious,
by the strength of our backs."

There is cheering,
there is always cheering.
The rivers are dark
and booming with life.

Col. Wolseley adjusts his collar,
thinks of his sacks of beans,
salt pork, flour, biscuit, tea.
He is not transgressing.
What he does
can only be right.

"Tell me, sergeant,"
he asks quietly,
"there's no one among us
who likes the French
or who loves the pope,
now is there?"

Beyond the woods
and the rapids
and the flies,
balmy Port Garry,
beguiling
on the Red River.

Garnet Wolseley,
emissary of empire,
finally at his destination,
empty
in the mud,
and suddenly,
in the awful rain.

"Out here," he shouts,
under a wet flag
to a straggle of soaking men,
"out here,
where the indians are,
even these wild people
in their fear, and in their flight,
have come to realize
who it is that is right."

Opaque Wolseley,
portent of history,
they fight his battle still.

Some Blats

is England green
is Tzara a dadaist
is tomorrow due soon
is money yellow
is love an illusion
is stillness silence
is the time right
is america there
is Barry really an island
is war needed
is money a failure
is black a colour
is the easywayout easy
is man an animal
is the poem finished
is yellow yellow
is true madness a gentle thing
is eternity locked up
is rock'n'roll here to stay
is the sun orange
is grass suitable for indoors
is moss small hair
is the Welsh language strong enough to carry a revolution
is the muse worthwhile
is the doctor really learned
is the Big Bopper on the right track
is laughter music
is sex and excuse
is sound holy
is death a disease
is rain too much
is rock'n'gravel news
is a cold a prison
is red out of date
is smoke silent
is the sky strong
is a toilet an amplifier
is the bluetone drunk

is the moon somewhere beyond america
is a tree a large flower
is petrol a sin in the sun
is carbon paper
is the sound of one hand clapping no more than silence
is venus false
is a monk brown throughout the year
is this time going to be the last time
is hope worth bothering about
is the answer to it all in a bottle
is tomorrow when it is all going to happen
is Wales free
is a whale free
is a wail free
is wine loud
is a vegetable sane
is paper thinkable
is a tank a table
is a running man a risk
is thunder the sound of the clouds bumping together
is fast a bulbous
is a lawnmower an object of beauty
is fire capable of creation
is a roll a weak rock
is a guitar an instrument of depth
is ink the only obliterator
is death the easy way out
is a gaz a stove
is metal heavy
is plastic alive
is blood forgotten
is air emulsified
is an ant a giant to a microbe
is an atom a star
is chess a product of bicycles
is seawater evil
is rubber hollow
is double vision the result of rainwater
is fishfood not really food
is the jaw no more than a door
is the head a hat

is music the lack of silence
is smoke filled with dreams
is distribution valid as an art
is fantasy voteable
is voltage a distant relation to the sky
is impact possible
is the hand a mountain
is really chuzz chuzz
is lipwork possage
is worthman plinleered
is it yungleit wooshez s
is jomp a leerkmmmp
is a distracktingor a brendingop
is a toomwow a yearnowf tort
is menmann gardes lompes gloop
is creakslis fanapzwash
is a salerang unda beatlum greal wow
is heartbustingflip le boutisgarg looplalaiy foor mee
is nonstlap finnslerg god
is flishfled flags
is wishta
is goerdistfl longongongham
is glad flijouy
is flomgsd flags
is fat lompnoph gus fat
is ghaj fgads westfring for
is hsfsdom slos tross ss
is flospssuu ususus s
is gadsas s
is flosdsd ss ssgss gs hsf
is testraljss tsssghdes ss dessss sssssjs sss
is sflossfgsssssjss sssss ssss sshgs
is ssssjs sss sssskss sssskss
is sssss ssss sssslss sss ss
is sss sssss sssss sss sssss s ss sssk
is ssss sssss sss ss sssss sss ss s
is s ssss sssssks ssss sssssss s ssssss
is s ss ssssssssss sssssssssss sss ssss
is s ssss sssss sssss s ss sssks sssss
is ss sssss ss sssssssssssss sssssss s sssss

18

is sss ssssssss sss ssss
is ssssssssss ssssss ssss sssssssss
is ssssssss ss sss ssssssssssssssssssk
is s ssssssssssssssssssssssssssssss ssss
is sss sssssssssssssssssssssss ssss
is s sssssssssssssss ssssssssss
is ss sssss ssss
is sssssssssssssss ssss
is s ssssssssssssssssssssssssssssssss
is ss ssssssssssssssssssksssssssssssssssssss
is s ssssssssssssssssssssssss sssssssss
is ss ssssssssssssssssssssssssssssssss
is s sssssssssssssssssssssssssssss
is s sssssssssssss
is ssssssssssssss
is sssssssssssksssss
is sssssssssssssssssss sssssssss
is sssssssssssssssssssssssssssss
is ssssssssssssssssssssssssssssssssss
is ssssssssssssssssssssssssssssssssss
is ssssssssssssssssssssssssssssssssss
is s sssssss sssssssssss
is ssssssssssssssssss
is ssssssssss sss
is ssssssssssssksss
is sssssssssssssssssssssssssss
is ssssssssssssssssssss
is ssssssss
is sssssssss
is ssssssss
is sssssss
is sssssssssssssssss
is ssssssssssssssssssssss
is ssssssssssssssssssss
issssssssssssssssssssssssss
isssssssssssssssss
issssssssssssssss
sssssssssssssss
sssssssssssssssssssssssssssssss
sssssssssssssssssssss
ssssssssssssssssss
s

The Death Of King Arthur Seen As A Recent War

On the airwaves we hear that General Belgrano has shells. They are pressed from hot metal, timewarped like black and white photographs, names chalked in shakey hand onto their sides. The governess tricks Menendez, makes him brag about his mirages, makes him think the sea is emulsified with enemy submarines. He sleeps with the girl without being aware of the deception. On awakening he is magnificently triumphant, parades in his quilted combat suit, inspecting troops. The son born of this union, Monsoonon, changes sides like an Italian. He is full of slow strength, his muscles cold, tautened by water.

The opening flights of the Vulcan imagine destruction in debilitating tracks along the runway. Radio messages are vague, trapped by an atmosphere thick as glue. They flew out of here, he says, his disembodied voice roughened, given urgency by it being on its own. I counted them out — Ban of Banoic, Lionel, Bors, Sons of Bors, Sons of Gaunes — and I counted them back.

The full story is bent like soft plastic. It fits the contours of the newscaster's head.

There is a decoy, wrecked by fire, devoid of men. It is a rendezvous for defenders, vulnerable, bobbing in unison around its bulk. They show pictures of it on the screen, radar-smears, smudges like space invaders. When it is hit again they forsake it, leave it and its coffins to the obliteration of the deep.

Menendez's conquering of the castle is his first great exploit after being dubbed a knight. He knows war, his men will tell you, it has stiffened him, given him grit, given him resolve. His enemies flounder, they splash. He has put them in water, darkly , their feet cemented in the coastal sea. His victories are silent, no one mentions them, no one writes them down.

Galahad flickers, sand in his wounds. At sea dark helicopters make themselves huge, stream stripped aluminium in elongated clouds. Nobleness turns to hauteur, hubris, leery smiles.

Towards the end there are references to episodes from history. Older dominions, seiged castles, dawn battles, the war in which Gawain himself has died. Trickles reach us, distortions, exaggerated pride. Sunk trawlers, snapped fuel vanes, looting, garbage, bleeding legs held together with iron-pins. The jumble is a high tide of flotsam, confused nomenclature, bad pictures, their sound dubbed out of sinc.

When the sky clears the faces are all still human; well-spoken, weather-beaten men. Their armour is heavy on the bog-land, their boots clank on the sparse metal of the roads. They have not been here long enough for pain to change them, for proximate death to age their eyes. At the end of transmission you can feel history altering. It spreads out with distance; reasons fragment, victories fade.

Strategic Targets

Depression Manifested Primarily in Physical Symptoms

In the committee room they were cold. The frosts had hurt the zinc which supported the glass over the light well. The panes were loose and the wind came in. The chairman was speaking quietly as if afraid the booming of his voice would damage something, shake the wall, knock the graffitied plaster into a chalky pile.

"Is it trouble they're afraid of then?"

His question hung limply, the remedial membership watched their hands, scratched their ears. In the distance a practise band thudded, someone near the door tapped a scruffy shoe.

"We'll protect them. Tell them we'll protect them. There'll be no trouble." He paused, "Carnival, what the hell are we celebrating, why do we aggravate things?"

No one spoke.

He watched them. He was used to it. He talked a lot to fill the silence, always leaving a chance for dialogue, even if it was never used.

The air was bitter. He looked down, scratched at a mark on the knee of his jeans. Shuffled, rubbed his nose. These strengths and forces he had around him — the grass roots alternative — in back rooms, and halls, and bars — what could they do to change anything? Shout a little. Draw some attention. Hope. Some would even pray. Lumpenproletariat motivated almost by chance. They had no power, they had no access to the means of power. They sat in their chairs and listened to events being planned, nodded, pulled the lobes of their ears. The silence creaked around him.

"So that is agreed," he said.

It Would Come In One Way Or Another

What do they call it?
lightning?
heat?
The yellow light before
you close your eyes?

22

To evidence our solidarity
I am considering use in all regions
employing both UK and US weapons
using primarily aircraft
and land-based missile systems.
The initial use would be restricted
to GDR, Czechoslovakia, Poland,
Romania, Hungary and Bulgaria.
Wetlands.
They need draining,
dig down,
let them boil and pour away.

Whenever a collision with the enemy
is probable,
and this probability will inevitably grow
commanders will, on their own initiative,
increase the number of rounds carried by each man.

Ability to see in the dark multiplies,
headlights down alleys,
flares above rooftops.
Objects are more visible when the moon
is behind the observer.
He may stand when he has a definite background
and should lie down when he has not.

I'll remain in the house,
take strength
from the news flickering on my television.
Their psychology will fill me.
I'll open my ears and heart to it,
I'll hold my children
and we'll think of God and we'll
pray and we'll listen to this voice
coming to us all the time down
through the wires and out into our
shaking room.

Calm it tells us.
Do not panic.
Victory is around the corner,
triumph is over the hill.

"Academic persons have little influence upon
political and military decisions, and
less than they suppose."

Lie on the floor.

Hold the walls.

The fire will not last for long.

Constantly In Action Since 1940

And I wonder, you know, what they trained me for, why I came
in the first place. Sort of an idealist I was I suppose. I had this
idea of devoting myself to helping others. You know, not
pussyfooting around but really helping people. I imagined myself in my uniform with my certificates, nicely framed, up on
the wall. There I'd be, dynamic, poised for action. The bell
would go and I'd be first on the scene, leaping from my
gleaming machine. And what does it turn out like? Stop. Ring
the door. Help them and their gammy legs or their bad backs or
their crippled hips.
"How are you today love?"
"Fine"
Hoist them into the back like parcels, deliver them, get them
checked and sprayed and touched and marked and whatever
else and then bundle them, flushed and tired and excited back

into the vehicle and drive them home again. Day in, day out. Same places, slowly changing faces.
"No Mrs Jones today, she went in the night."
"Oh yes."
You get the odd bit of excitement now and again. A road crash or whatever, but mostly its routine. You spend a lot of time picking your nails. Now and again someone is sick in the back. Gives you a chance to show your skills. Throw water on it, bash it with a mop. Last week we had some inspector from the government round. Counted us and our ambulances, ticked his clipboard. Gave us all a mask. Keep them in the cabs at all time, vital he said. We had a lesson in pulling them on and pulling them off. Like divers we were. Some of the old men said it was like this in the war. Bombers droning over, cowering there in a tin shack with your gas mask in your sweating palm. Gas masks. What are they expecting? I thought the next lot was all to do with bombs.

There are Many Ways Of Rising

practise advancing noiselessly on roads
try it on your toes
wrap rags round the studs of your boots
do it slowly
and in various formations
over open ground
whispering your words
hardly breathing your commands.

The following are vital
observe them

When moving in short grass or on hard ground
the toe should touch the ground first and the
foot be raised higher than normally

In long grass the pace should be slow and
the heel be placed on the ground before the toe

25

Precautions should be taken to prevent
equipment rattling

Do not clash against other men.
Your men.
Watch them
when you can.

doors smashed and curtains torn
plate glass gone
internal doors forced
gas heaters broken
piano smashed
floor tiles ripped up
filing cabinets forced
rear doors and windows broken
fireplace pulled out from wall
internal firedoors wrenched off
stair carpet ripped up
personal effects damaged
stereo system broken
bed overturned and casters broken
chair covers slashed
television and furniture smashed
light fittings pulled out
gas pipe fractured
outside toilet bowl broken
personal effects devastated
mirrors smashed
bed base broken and thrown in garden
food scattered
radio smashed
settee and bed mattress torn open
dressing table broken
wardrobe doors torn off
shelves ripped out
clothes scattered around room.

Keep your heads boys
do it when they're out
do it at dawn
observe all the cautions
suppleness, lightness, ease of movement
flow over
round
and under them.
Show them that in this white land
their barbarity
will not be tolerated.

Their inner-city colonization
never wins.

Our Ideals Rather Than Self Indulgence

Later he watched leaflets scatter up the street. Exhortations
blowing like leaves, collecting in a murkey froth around the
wheels of cars. It was a dulled atmosphere, a residue of
inaction. Dusk with faint radio and distant traffic. He looked up
at the Victorian facade of the former registry office. It was as
he had expected, further damage, further decay. The terrace
had been converted in the heady days of the hippies into a
centre for advice and freedom. The ensuing decade had brutal-
ized it, scarred, made it an emblem for an age of intimidation.
The ornate window surround had been smashed revealing a
nexus of lath and crumbled stone. The window boards were
cracked, ripped, overpainted with the arbitrary names of local
bands. He watched a scruffy dog sniff the ripple of debris
washed up like a tide mark around the door.

Further along the isolated wreckage of a single car smouldered.
It lay in a patch of oil, messed by water, blackening the road. It
reminded him of war films. The top end of the street was a
morass of smashed glass. It lay like ice, a mixture of granular
windshield fragments and longer, jagged shards. Shopfronts
missing, rows of vehicles with their windows busted in.

He looked for someone he knew but there was nobody. His
day had been emptied like water down a filthy drain.

Severe Stress

The local crises are survived.

"she listened but did not hear"

I blame
I blame
I blame
I blame
I blame
I blame

Bouts, Recurring

Grasp the grenade in the throwing hand
no gloves, no rings,
with the fingers holding the lever tight
against the body
tremble, let the blood flush under your nails,
pull out the arming pin,
do not relax grip on the lever before throwing.
Throw.
Throw.
Throw.
Throw.
Do not wait for the whites of their eyes
these lepers will come at you
wearing towels
wearing masks.
They will be gesticulating,
they will be shouting.
Stand your ground
Grit your teeth.
They are angry children
with scabs on their hands.
Throw.
Throw.

Drum your shield.
Do not run.
They have become habituated to the threat.

"Bastille 1789, Kronstadt 1921, Barcelona 1937,
Watts 1965, Paris '68, Portugal '74, Egypt,
Soweto, Poland '76, Kabul, Amsterdam, Copenhagen '80,
Poland, Zurich, Brixton '81.....
The Fire next-time will enflame all our passions and burn
all our states."

There are no special zones
There are no exempt classifications
There are no arrangements,
no agreements, no measures.

Hold your eyes boys,
hold them until they melt.

Mass Dispersal

He was on the mud banks. Soft like jelly. Brown, glutenous, shiney, intestine split open, trickled with rabid water. The grass and reeds had all gone, burned, crumbled, grown wild and huge like green christmas baloons, burst in a flash of infected sap, a sludge of brown fibres marking the river's edge.

It was some months since anyone had been here. He guessed it rather that knew it. He coughed. His lungs burned. He spat a small quantity of discoloured spittle onto the ground, wiped his mouth with the brown back of his hand. Ahead of him was the beach. Sand seeped with oil, freckled with the white bellies of fish. He moved towards them, slowly, drawn inexorably by the sea.

This place had never been much, the last bay on the coast before the docklands began. A few hundred yards of mucky sand, a cafe, a jetty for small boats, for fishermen and their cans of wriggling grubs and tiny worms.

He remembered being there surrounded by the squall of gulls, the shriek of children, the thrash of waves. There was little now, a sombre sea pressing a scummy shore.

Peace. He gritted his teeth. Aye, peace.

He clambered the rocks, stumbled, half-fell, reached the edge of the sand. There were bones, grey rags. He skirted them. The beach had become crowded in the last days. Half crazed people, like lemmings in desperation plunging at the waves. They wanted the salt, the water to cleanze them. To take all the flames from out of their souls. They had died in their hundreds. Half sunk in sand, their flappy mouths filled with sea. He looked across them, saw the remains of an ambulance — its red lettering still showing faintly as it rusted back into the coastline. Old gas masks littered the high tide line. False hopes, filtering death till they burst.

He could have cried, stamped his feet at the uselessness. But he didn't. He was too tired, too frail. The dusk was coming. He wanted all his energy for the sea. He touched his forehead, felt the bone flex sponge-like under his finger. He looked west, watched the brightness fade. Like the lemmings before him he staggered, continued on his way.

Gertrude Stein, Doing It Again.

— a permutation —

ts tog ting
tr   ting
ting
t tud tag
tag ten
tag ts tint
tat
    tevt tevt
tawfully tsss
ting what
tevery it
ting ting
ten tag tag
tsst ting
tevt tint
tag tint
tint tint
tint tint tag
ting one again and
ting ruble tag ten
trest it again tag
tout about
toot it
tout about it
tevery ting one
again ting
tat tag
tevery ting
      ting it
fully everybody it
tag it
tout it
about it
tag know you trouble
ting tint interest
         ting

that is what
tog
tag about it
do it again
do it again
that is whatog
again
ting again
do it again
awfully gain
do it again
do it again
and it is not interesting
ten tout again
then you know you are again
touting anything
awfully
everything
everything everything again
tag again
tag again
tag everything doing anything
everything having done anything
again. Do it again.
And you do it again.
Everybody does everything
anything doing anything
again. Do it again.
You know you are doing it again,
again.
You do it again,
you do it again.
Then awfully, anything,
everything troubled
everything worried about anything
again.
you know
ten tag tog again and again and again

Its not interesting

go on doing anything
because everyone worries
That is what everybody worries about
again and again and again
then you know anyone'll do anything
it is awfully hard for anything
having done anything, everything
and you do it again
and want to do it again.
You want to do it again?
You do it again,
you do it again,
and naturally you are troubled by it
you are doing it again
getting troubled by it
and its not interesting
again, not interesting
go on doing anything because it's not interesting
that is what everybody worries about
then you know
it is awfully hard for anyone to
go on doing anything because
everyone is troubled by everything.
Having done anything
you naturally want to do it again
and if you do it again
then you know you are doing it again
and its not interesting.
That is what everybody worries about.

I wanted this piece to have a title which mentioned Warsaw and the Ghetto and perhaps connotated the press, the illegal press. But all these terms mean something else now. I won't bother. It starts like this:_

You should not know and should not ask,
don't procrastinate
don't name, never name,
keep quiet, no one knows
but you know, only you.
listen:
        all the time the water running,
        rolling together, confluencing,
        swelling out from the thickness of your arm
        to the size of your thigh. Large it's large.
        It make more noise. It goes
        splaartsch splartsch splartsch
        teeeeeerch tugha tugha tugha ta tug
        when it goes fast it wobbles, knocks
        the rocks about. You can watch them if
        you get close enough, they make
        little lines of force in the
        clear rolling grey.
It's reliable,
no substitutes,
you must do it yourself, alone
if you happen to know, keep quiet
don't inquire
hold the paper
you are trusted
don't make notes,
don't write things down.

        back of hands, envelopes, slivers from the edges
        of packets, endpapers, napkins, luggage tags,
        clothes pegs where the knife has whittled
        the surface clean.
        What else can you write on. Don't inquire.

There are people whose fear can only be assuaged by words.
People whose fear shakes the spittle and tongue around so
much they cannot speak. These people record it, the fears,
purge it from their systems by spelling it, putting it down. I
don't think they are literators, necessarily. I mean they don't
write novels, stories, they are not really that kind of creative
men. How do they do it what it is that they do? I don't know. I
can't. I couldn't. I'd sit down and worry it round me until I went
dizzy. These people are stronger. Their death becomes touch-
able. I don't know them but because of them I do.

Who can be a reader?
who is known well.
Keep quiet, you can betray —
but not everyone can.
Don't talk in the street.
You must not make notes,
code it, destroy it,
the less said, keep quiet,
if you happen to know, keep quiet
don't inquire,
keep quiet,
only you know
you are the one,
don't receive, who can,
not everyone,
keep quiet,

> I used to think about it often,
> all the time, think about it. When
> they took a middle aged man and asked
> him, got him to mark ticks on a form
> they found his thoughts turned to sex once
> every 7 minutes. At least. I used
> to think about this more than that. Sit thinking
> about it, walk thinking about it, read thinking about
> it, trailing off, leaving it there between the
> lines.

Who can be a reader?
who is known well
keep quiet, you can betray,

not everyone can
Do it. Destroy it.
less said
never mention
quiet
no one
quiet
quiet

They all kept quiet, kept quiet, kept bloody quiet.
That's what they did. Self effacing. Silence.
ssss   tssss   sssss
snikerterr
            tsssss
They make body sounds. Sound of bone,
air through fluid, feet in old
shoes, creaking, worn soles shuffling, dust.
They made those sounds. Tssss sounds.
They go   tssssss oow   tsssssssoow
tuka tuka tuka tukatukatukatukta tsssssoow
tuka tuka tuka tukatukatukatukata tsssssssoow
tsssssoooooooow

They don't make anything, dust doesn't
make anything, ash doesn't make anything,
except smudged water, rippled, slowly,
long sheets where the rain pits it,
snickers it, thickens it, gives it motive force.
Then it talks again, when it moves.
It goes splaartsch splartsch splartsch
splaartsch tsch tsch.
This stream with the ash in it,
raked in it, taking it away.

And all the time I used to think about it
all the time before that.
If you happen to know, keep quiet,
don't inquire

I used to think about it
hot mornings, sun behind me, thats why they wrote it down.

I wasn't there. What am I supposed to do?
Remember what they wrote, what it cost them,
when they wrote it, what it was.
Korczak and his children, two hundred orphaned children,
marched on the hot morning, warm paving, sun on
their backs. All of them ordered, subdued, each holding a
little bag with a flask of water and a
piece of bread. Cloth bag on a piece of string.
They entered the Umschlagplatz, scrubbed,
hair flat, clean clothed, four by four, four by four.
And Korczak, wasted, bent and hatless, in front of
them, old man, guardian, their protector, broken by force,
by fear. There was nothing he could do.
They loaded on the freight cars, these children,
in order, in silence, with their procession
snaking, so slightly, quiet.   They did
as they were told, these orphans, jewish, quiet.
You have to be clean for Treblinka, you have to be quiet.
Who could not think about it?
tsch tsch
tsch tsch
What do you want me to do?
Make the sound they make?
I can't make the sound they make.
I don't know
I don't ask.
all there is
is the water
tsch wobbling
grey white, grey white
grey grey
grey grey.

Note

Instantaneous Magnetism and *Bright Wind* are ultimately works of processed quotation. They use material both excavated and found, both amended and raw. They are beyond concrete. They take Clark Coolidge's position where he argues against "the rack of words a writer would have behaviourally" preferring to tap the myriad external sources available to all. They are a process outside argument, like digging earth, like sweeping up gravel from the edge of the road.

Taped versions of both poems have been made. *Bright Wind*, pioneered at Chris Torrance's writing class was included on Balsam Flex's *Dances Interdites* produced by Eric Vonna-Michel and *Instantaneous Magnetism*, finalized in the Wentwood forest, was included by Phil Mailard on one of his Stone Lantern cassette anthologies.

Instantaneous Magnetism

Magnetism is a charm, not an annoyance

tless   resurge
call   resway
restlessly   social
restless   studness
rest   onless
such   less
resevere   gain
sillless   rest
sinsome   sere

Face motions. Various kinds.
        especially the tongue
        upper
             weakness
        small matters
          habit

magnetism is a power

they twirl
they rub against themselves
they open and shut
they are interlaced
they spread
they stroke the face
they caress the nose

women   scream   sighing   this   like   yawning
usual   respirations   halting   speech   hundred   talks
speaks   without   speaking   formally   speak   smoothly
gossipy   talk   rapid   talker   much   talk
the   orator   is   speaking   few   words
you   talk   talk   some   and   talk
body   sighs   mere   gush   person   speaks
rapid   talk   talk   is   who   talks
like   yawning   open   like   mouth   breathing
four   repeat   aloud   get   volume   which
open   throat   speech   charged   place   membrane
singing   common   translated   tone   feel   voice
vocal   fault   swallow   note   barking   spoke
modulations   guttural   too   talking   drifting   repels
pitch   down   note   time   preached   preached
pitch   relief   vibrations   as   talking   range
highest   silence   silence   silence   silence   silence

39

```
b d
  //////                          //////
  //////                           //////
   //////                           //////
     //////                          //////
      //////                          //////
       //////                          //////
  //////    b d                        //////
  //////                                //////
    //////                              //////
    //////                              //////
     //////                              //////
       //////                        //////  //////
  b                                //////  //////
    //////                        //////  //////
   //////                        //////  //////
     //////                    //////  //////
      //////                  //////  //////
     //////                //////  //////
    //////              //////  //////
     //////          //////  //////
      //////      //////  //////
       //////  //////  //////
        //////////  //////
     //////  //////
   //////  //////
  //////  //////  //////
 //////  //////  //////
  //////      //////  //////
  //////        //////  //////
  //////          //////  //////
 //////  bb'd
 //////    bb'd bb'd
 //////    bb'd bb'd bb'd
 //////      bb'd bb'd
 //////    b'dst d'dst
 //////          b'dst
 //////    b'dst b'dst b'dst
  //////        b'dst b'dst
   //////        b'dst b'dst
    //////      bidst bb'st d'dst
   //////          ddl'st  ddl'st
   //////                    //////
   //////                   //////
    //////                  //////
     //////                  //////
      //////                  //////
       //////                //////
```

enemi   magnetism

magnetism   turn

magnetism   charm

tude   magnetism

Way. Magnetism

electrici   magnetism

magnetism   brain

magnetism

magnetism   s

magnetism t   lps

magnetism,   nd   re

magnetism,

generate magnetism

without magnetism

endowed   magnetism

diffuse   magnetism

collect   magnetism

anima   magnetism

Thus many

from the

atomic

is the union

in

we do not

developing

'

tism, they

nal   net

nat   tis

king   mag   m,

as a study

sup   stucture

the enemies of

m
m
m
m
m
mmm
m
m
mm
m
m
m
mmm
m
m
m
m
mm
mmm
agne

the one hand will move
while the other is held still
tt
t
tt
t
t
ttis is
s
s
s
ism
mmm
m
m
m
m
m

look,   how it steals
patines;   bright gold
look,   how the floor
free   host   liberty

it's twenty years

. . . .
    . . dwr . . .
. . . . .
      . . . d . .
. . . .
      . . . . .
    . . . disg . .
        . . .
        . . .
    gyn . . .
    . nn . .
    . . . .
. . . .
. . .

something will hitch

maddnd   widnd   broadnd
stiffld   muffld   baffld
quaffst   stuffst
fifths   twelfths

gld
        gld
    gld
            gld
        gld
    gld
            gld
    gld
            gld
        gld
            gld
gld
            gld
            gld
                gld
    gld
        gld
            tackl
                        st buckldst
            encircl
                        st   beck   nst t
                t
                    t
            t
                            engulfed
        lft lft
        lft lft
    lft
43

floated
                    the water
flat
rose leaf
changing
full   extra full
floating
added,   reversed
out front
out full

men and men and upright and sweet
and these and is and these and
continued and who and they and men
and dark and any and also and then
and then and it and gain and the
and then and then and then

"Tie tight
  sunshine"

KAMSKT
KAMSTK
IRKUTSK

Bright Wind

Here are a few
((((heal))))
        ing
from his mother's
((((perfect)))

((((ing))))   ness
((((great))))

spiritual
examples of the
man lame

womb
((((unanim))))
in their approach

many other heroines
but no early record

((((unwill))))
Believe.
Danger.

The evangalist ((((preach)))) ed for more
than an hour
everynight you shine so bright
wuz um ah
     bulum um ah
boomboom bulum ah
     meestar moon
do   oo   do
do   oo   do
do   oo   do
        aaah py
any more

My dad lived as if God didn't exist
lost weekends
no longer potent
((((transform)))) ation

ritzee there as I could bee.

bodla
        owow
bodla
        owow
((((bod))))
      ((((a))))
   ((((ow))))
        ((((ow))))
   ((((bodla))))
((((bompbomp udla ah))))
  ((((ah))))
      ((((ah))))
        ((((reever))))
          ((((bom'))))
        ((((bomp))))
              ((((owow))))
              ((((bb))))
            ((((bah))))
                  ((dudla la))
                ((la lar)))

      ((dudlala))
                    la

tongues and prophecy
cautious and wise
praising and glorifying
movement and mountains
interpreter and in
good and intelligible
loosed and mouths
strength and fulness
nonmembers and females

motives and desires
gas and electric
rushing and struggling
faith and godly
distinct and convincing
strenuous and occasional
week and many
bed and found
uneasy and disturbed
methods and results
city and people
frowned upon and imitated
fingers and bade
life and opportunity
god and they

sinners in the hands

((((bom   bom))))
    ((((buda))))
   ((((dum))))
          ((((dum))))
    ((((b))))
          ((((om))))
      ((((b))))
             ((((om))))

For ten days
skies an estimated
imagining that
he asked
                    under
                    70
                    they
the open
thousand heard
must have misunderstood

he asked
"from   eye
  omm my door"

ran through the streets and was chased
ran through the streets drumming
ran through the streets, warm wet
they will see visions

(((((ah))))
(((((ah))))
 (((((ah)))))
        (( ))
          (((( ))))
         (((( ))))
           (((( ))))
            ( )
           (( ))
            ( )
           (((( ))))
           (((( ))))
             ((( )))
            (((( ))))
         ((ah))
         ((ah))
         ((((ah))))
(((ah)))
   (((ah)))
          LORD

hal
al
el
al
oo woo
oo woo
j
oo woo
ah

the spiritual gifts were no longer observed
laughter
no barrier

```
pru    den    cia         Dam    bor    ien
oin    pra    din         coe    Dem    bur
bar    uon    pre         don    cui    Dim
Dom    ber    aun         pri    dun    cao
ceu    Dum    bir         ean    pro    dan
den    cia    Dam         bor    (le))  pru
din    coe    (le))       bur    oin    pra
don    cui    Dim         bar    uon    ((le)))
dun    cao    Dom         (le))  aun    pri
                                 ((((ee))))
                                      ((((e))))
                            ((((e))))
                                        ((((e))))
                                     ((ee))
                                          ((ee))

                                  (e)


                                      (e)
```

for the most parts scorn and derision
she firmly believed
she couldn't be turned
she wouldn't look
she held tight
she held hard

115 under Polycarp
                (((( ))))
115 - 200
130 asserted
130 - 200
154 As late
154 North Africa
185 diminishing signs
220 esteemed

250 ordered government officials
254),
313 General and violent
367 that they were fully
1231 the monk
1419 Xavier
1552 and others
1685 the Camisards
1738 Wesley
1833 published a refutation
1834 at 42
1874 in Round Lake
was 1888
1893 and 1900
1896 manifestations
1897 after a succession
1901 he succumbed
1903 the near blind eye
1905 and the exodus
1906 — three
1909 the same size
1910.
1912 then World War
(((( ))))
     (())
1914 heralding the message across
1948 to 1956
1948 failed to invite black
mid 1950s
1952 to 8174
1952 inside cover
1954 a short middle age
1957 seem prophetic
1958.
1959 witness and chat
by 1959
1960s
1961 explained why members were so friendly

1962 he met Fidel Castro
1963 to 645,000
1964 yielding Glossolalia
1967 it was taller than any other building
1968 indicator
1970 18 million dollars
                ((( ))))
1971 accreditation granted
1971 [18]

                (((())))

        ((
)

            (((

    Then
         calm
    full
         business
((( )))
    men walk.

*If Marcel Duchamp had been writing this he would
have put it in the loft for six months to let it secrete
and have things attach. But it's not as casual as that.
It's the kind of thing that the structuralists are said to
like, writing about writing. And I've always hated
that. So it isn't, its about art and if it's not that then
it's something else altogether, it's about building
sheds.*

blue light, blue light, blue light
continuous light
animal light, garage light,
mechanical, plastic,
predominantly red,
predominantly silver.
art, predominantly blue,
yellow blue, yellow blue
light polyphonic, polyrhythmic,
predominantly indispensable, pictorial,
it whirls, cones, spirals,
it rolls, rolls, tangles:

You get to thinking about concepts, everyone does it, thinks
conceptually. You get these ideas flashing around like little bits
coming off the end of a welder's torch. You've seen it, watched
them, white things, showering. Bright then not bright. Think
about them. They crackle quietly then they don't make any
noise.
This is it. It's where it starts. Here.
Predominantly light.
But it's what you have to do next that fools you, where it gets
difficult. Craft. It's what you've got to do. Making. All this
trimming around with a chisel and a cool paint brush. Moulding.
You must do it, got to do.

Gradually we eliminate the future,
us painters,
make it special, make it whole.
We incorporate volumes and colours,
a kind of obscurity
which becomes our canvas,
our states of mind, our noises,
our pure findings, railway stations,

ports, garages bubbling elipses,
concave, convex, spherical,
spiral, excessively pale and drooping,
the transcendency of what we do.

I'm not making myself clear. I know I'm not. I can tell. What I
mean is this::–
Its a hot day and when I find his studio he's inside. Collecting
pencils. He does it all the time. Walks around with his eyes on
the ground, bumps into things, cracks his glasses, you can see
the knot of cellotape on the bridge, collecting dirt. He has
hundreds of them. Pens, pencils, mangled, leaked, thrown
away things. They come from the gutter now. He writes them
down. Goes around hunting, finding them, laying them out in
lines. He shows me a book where he's got all bits of slogans
and names and writings off the pens listed. Times and dates
and places where he found them. "It's like a poem," I say, "I
could chant it." He shakes his head. He has them set in pews
like a church, like the big head of a rocket. He fixes them, looks
at them, reads them. Paints on the wood around them, gouges,
manipulates. All the clips are in straight parallels. All the time
he's talking, holding scraps of things, bricks, bits of metal,
rocks, papers, tubes of paint. He takes it further, he doesn't
leave it, he hardly ever does. I ask him. "Occasionally. Mostly I
work," he says, "keep touching, push the concept along."

Vertical lines are dead lines
force is involved
plastic passionless, static harmoniousness
desires, mysterious fascination
tactile shouts, reds, polenta yellows,
saffron yellows, brass sounds,
lines, volumes, colours, lines.
These are the theatres, music-halls, cinemas,
brothels, garages, hospitals, workshops.
They are triangular, ellipsoidal, oblong, conical
They carouse, they go
reeeeeooooooooooooooooooooo churn churn
churn tssch flap flap flap
                flap flap flap
                flap flap flap
                flap flap flap
                flap flap flap

53

Lots of times its fussy, always too fussy,
endless, endless rolling and smoothing and rounding
and rounding. When you get involved you sit with the
thing for days. You stare at it. Blind it. 6 weeks
for one line, ragged when it comes. I use a morning to
change a word. Then I think. Then I change it back.
Rounding. All the crackles, smudges, shadows made bland.
Wiped until they go translucent. You can hardly see them
anymore. Why? I can't tell you. I'm building sheds,
digging out a hole for hardcore, flat concrete base. You
can see them when you've done. Nailed wood and creosote,
doors on big hinges, long nosed vees. If it's solid and
you've made the roof right then they last. You can use
them often when the last.

The silences are static, yellow arabesques.
They are noise, speed, chaos, vibration.
They are the sounds of railway stations,
stadiums, restaurants, cafes.
They are the sounds of women, they are green, blue, light blue.
They jump, dance, exaggerate,
clash, contrast.
They are grey, brown, muddy,
pure horizontal, bombastic,
serene, an intellectual rhythmic quadrature.

You know what I'm doing. I've told you.
Smoothing, planing, rubbing, rolling.
Each time I look at it its less,
smaller, rounder,
like a pebble you've had in your mouth and kept in your pocket
and taken out and sucked and rolled under your tongue and
spat out and dried on your shirt and put back in your pocket and
thought about and then tried sucking without it and felt what
its absence might mean and touched it, the actual pebble, with
your fingers at the same time, niggled it a bit, down near where
the rip in the material at the bottom of the pocket is, so the
pebble touched your skin, not too sharp because you've soft-
ened it, not cold, and you take it out, palming it, suck it again.
It's like that.

Nobody told me.
That's what I'm doing,
no more,
just that.

Vicki Slowe studied at the London College of Fashion and at the Camden Arts Centre (Printmaking).

In 1982 she was elected as a Fellow of The Royal Society of Painters, Etchers and Engravers. In that year she was also elected a member of the Printmakers Council.

First published in 1984
by Rivelin Grapheme Press
24 Aireville Road, Frizinghall, Bradford BD9 4HH

Copyright © Peter Finch 1984

Printed in England by Tony Ward and typeset by Bryan Williamson at the Arc & Throstle Press, The Old Fire Station, Rochdale Road, Todmorden, Lancs.

British Library Cataloguing in Publication Data

Finch Peter
    Some music and a little war.
    I. Title
    821'.914   PR6056.147

    ISBN 0-947612-05-X

This edition consists of 600 copies of which twenty-six copies have been lettered A-Z and signed by the author.

Rivelin Grapheme Press
London & Bradford 1984